A *DISCOVER* BOOK

come to the
mountain
with me

TWO CHILDREN ENJOY GOD'S CREATION

By Mary Carpenter Reid

Illustrated by June Goldsborough

ISBN 0-8066-2631-3   LCCN 92-73011

Manufactured in the U.S.A.   AF 9-2631

96   95   94   93   92   1   2   3   4   5   6   7   8   9   10

Augsburg
MINNEAPOLIS

For marvelous Michael

When my cousin came to visit me, we made *big* plans.

Each day we—
   hiked to the end of my block,
   skipped to the end of the park,
   climbed a rock and up a hill,
   and jogged until we got all out of breath.
Then we walked back to my home on my block
. . . getting ready.

We gathered up stacks to put in our packs:
a folded tent,
a shovel,
lots of rope,
some tissues and towels,
a cake of soap,
a compass,
a whistle to blow.
Those stacks really began to grow
when we added food we wanted to take
and two tin cups that wouldn't break.
Then we had to fit it all in our packs
. . . getting ready.

We put our sleeping bags on top and tied them
so they wouldn't flop.
We stepped on the scales with all that stuff
to check if our packs were light enough
. . . getting ready.

One evening, for practice,
my cousin and I put on our packs and—
 hiked to the end of my block,
 skipped to the end of the park,
 climbed a rock and up a hill,

and walked until we got back to my home
on my block,
where we slept out in the yard all night long.
Then we were ready . . .
for a backpacking trip in the mountains!

I took my cousin to *see* the mountain that God made—
a big, big, enormous mountain
that wore an enormous, leafy green sweater
made of tree tops,
with buttons of polished gray stones.
The mountain reached so high in the sky,
it got kisses from clouds passing by.

We began to climb up-up-up.

A deer *saw* us.
It stood still as a statue,
stiller than trembling leaves
on the Aspen trees—watching us.
Then suddenly, the deer—and we didn't know why—
raced by in a flicker of feet
and a whirlwind of dust, passing us.
And right before our eyes, that deer disappeared.

I took my cousin to *hear* the mountain that God made.
A sudden breeze rushed through the trees,
whistling a marching tune.
We walked faster, fast as the breeze.
We were a marching band.
Our packs jingled and jangled,
our boots scraped and scuffed,
our breath huffed and puffed,
and we clapped our hands,
as we climbed up-up-up.

A bunch of jays *heard* our marching band.
They flitted and fussed and swooped over us,
squawking like they were talking, teasing us,
  Hurry up, you slowpokes! Don't stop!
  It's easy to get to the top.
"Of course," we said, "when you have wings."

I took my cousin to *smell* the mountain that God made—
Christmas smells—from real Christmas trees,
   growing crisp and pointy all around us.
Funny smells—a whiff of vanilla from the trunk
   of a tall Jeffrey Pine.
Our own smells—of mosquito lotion on our skin
   and warm, dusty clothes.

We climbed up-up-up.

At twilight, when we got quiet,
curious animals came and *smelled* us
and all the good things we brought to eat.
They peeked at us from back in the brush,
waiting, planning to get a special treat.
But we fooled them.
We tossed a rope around a tree limb
and tied our packs high above the ground.

Then, we snuggled in our tent and whispered our prayers.
We said good night to the stars so bright
and the moon so light.
And absolutely everything felt right.

I took my cousin to *taste* the mountain that God made.

We fixed a trail breakfast.
There was no refrigerator, no sink, no table.
But we mixed water with yellow powder for scrambled eggs,
and we mixed water with orange powder for tangy juice.
We nibbled on salty beef jerky
and pieces of sweet, dried apple.
It was better than breakfast at home.
And after we'd eaten as much as we were able,
we remembered to pick up our trash,
leaving nothing behind for anyone to find.
Not a trace—anyplace.

And we climbed up-up-up.

More ants than anybody could count
chewed on an ancient, crumbling log—busy, busy.
More bees than anybody could count
tasted blossoms in a lily patch—buzzing, buzzing.

We followed tracks near a stream,
hoping to find some giant creature
that no one else knew about.
A fat, bushy tail waved from behind a rock,
but wouldn't come out.
So we went back to the trail where ants were still chewing,
and the bees still buzzing.

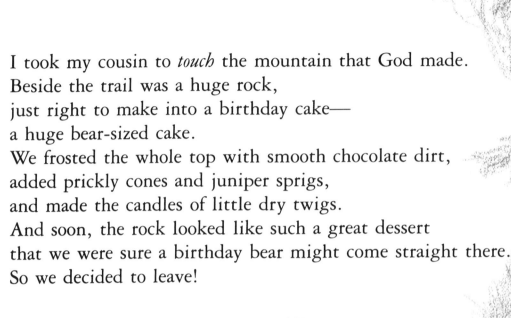

I took my cousin to *touch* the mountain that God made.
Beside the trail was a huge rock,
just right to make into a birthday cake—
a huge bear-sized cake.
We frosted the whole top with smooth chocolate dirt,
added prickly cones and juniper sprigs,
and made the candles of little dry twigs.
And soon, the rock looked like such a great dessert
that we were sure a birthday bear might come straight there.
So we decided to leave!

At last we reached the end of the trail.
We tiptoed out on gray granite stone
and looked down on an airplane flying by.
Strong winds from far below *touched* our faces
and swept across an old pine tree
that grew, twisted and tired and kneeling on the stone.

My cousin and I stood on the mountain,
higher than the valleys, higher than meadows.
We stood on the mountain almost alone.

When we hiked back down the trail, we—
    Had *seen* the mountain.
    Had *heard* the mountain.
    Had *smelled* the mountain.
    Had *tasted* the mountain.
    Had *touched* the mountain.

We had stood on the top almost alone—
we and the old pine tree.

But God travels with my cousin and me,
and that makes it nice to sometimes be almost alone.